WARRIOR SCIENCE

GLADIATOR
Science

Armour, Weapons and Arena Combat

by Allison Lassieur

raintree

a Capstone company — publishers for children

Raintree is an imprint of Capstone Global Library Limited, a company incorporated in England and Wales having its registered office at 264 Banbury Road, Oxford, OX2 7DY – Registered company number: 6695582

www.raintree.co.uk
myorders@raintree.co.uk

Text © Capstone Global Library Limited 2017
The moral rights of the proprietor have been asserted.

Edited by Aaron Sautter
Designed by Steve Mead
Picture research by Pam Mitsakos
Production by Steve Walker
Originated by Capstone Global Library Limited
Printed and bound in China

Capstone Press would like to thank Josh Davis of Davis Reproductions for his assistance in creating this book.

ISBN 978 1 474 71124 1
20 19 18 17 16
10 9 8 7 6 5 4 3 2 1

British Library Cataloguing in Publication Data
A full catalogue record for this book is available from the British Library.

Acknowledgements
Alamy: INTERFOTO, 19, Jochen Tack, 21; Bridgeman Images: Bianchetti/Leemage, 26, De Agostini Picture Library/G. Dagli Orti, 24–25, Look and Learn, 13; Dreamstime: Microstock77, cover background, 22–23 bottom background; Getty Images: Ann Ronan Pictures/Print Collector, 29, Doug Pearson, 10, Nicolas Moulin Photography, 9, Prisma/UIG, 5; iStockphoto: oscar_killo, 28, Sylphe_7, 17 top right; Newscom: akg-images/Peter Connolly, 16 bottom middle, Photo by Guy Bell/REX Shutterstock (4931217ba), 8; Shutterstock: 3drenderings, 17 left, bkp, right cover, Dmytro Zinkevych, left cover, 11, Eky Studio, cover background, design element throughout book, Fotokvadrat, 23 top, Luis Louro, 6–7, back cover, Nebojsa Kontic, cover bottom left, 22, Nejron Photo, 14–15, Paul B. Moore, cover bottom middle, Pranann, 16 middle right, Santi0103, cover bottom right; Thinkstoc

Every effort has been m   luced in this book. Any
omissions will be rectifi   publisher.

All the internet address   of going to press.
However, due to the dyr   ave changed, or sites
may have changed or ce   d publisher regret
any inconvenience this   hanges can be
accepted by either the a

CONTENTS

SCIENCE: TO THE DEATH!

The two gladiators stood face to face. Their bodies dripped with sweat and blood. The men circled each other, careful to avoid the slick, dark blood from earlier battles. Each warrior sized up his opponent … when would he make his move? How hard would he hit? Which way would be best to dodge when he attacks?

Suddenly one man lunged forward to attack. But he leaned in too far and lost his balance. Unfortunately, his opponent saw the mistake. He slashed the stumbling warrior with a lightning-fast sword strike. The unlucky gladiator went down in a pool of blood. The Emperor smiled as the victorious warrior waved to the crowd.

For Roman gladiators, success in combat depended on more than strong weapons. Science was just as important as a sharp sword. For the winning warrior above, speed was a deciding factor. Being faster than his opponent helped him achieve victory. Ancient Roman gladiators relied a lot on science during their battles. Using the science behind their weapons and combat skills often meant the difference between life and death.

To survive and succeed in the arena, Roman gladiators relied on the science behind their armour, weapons and combat training.

CHAPTER ONE

PROTECTED BY SCIENCE

➡ Gladiators knew every day could be their last. Two things stood between them and death: their armour and science. Gladiators may not have realized it, but they relied a lot on the **physics** of their armour in battle.

Staying alive with physics

A gladiator's armour was his first line of defense. Metal armour didn't just keep a warrior from getting cut with a sword. When a weapon hit a gladiator's armour, the blow released a lot of energy. The armour worked to **disperse** that energy across its surface so the warrior's body didn't absorb it. Most armour was also made with smooth, rounded shapes that helped **deflect** weapons. This design made it difficult for enemies to connect with a solid blow.

physics science that studies matter, energy, force and motion

disperse to spread out over a wide area

deflect to cause something to go in a different direction

Gladiators also carried shields made of bronze or iron. Their shields were great at blocking and deflecting heavy blows from strong weapons. A skilled gladiator could even use his shield to knock an opponent off balance, which gave him a big advantage in a fight.

 Heavy shields were also useful for absorbing and dispersing the energy from weapon blows.

Heavyweight gladiators

Gladiators were divided into heavyweight and lightweight classes based on their size and strength. Heavyweight gladiators included *secutors* and *murmillos*. They wore metal armour and carried large shields. Their heavy armour provided good protection. But it slowed them down and exposed them to attacks from faster opponents.

SECUTOR

SECUTOR MEANS "CHASER". THIS HEAVY GLADIATOR'S JOB WAS TO CHASE DOWN AND DEFEAT HIS OPPONENTS BEFORE HE BECAME TOO TIRED.

HELMET
The secutor's helmet was smooth and round. It included a wide guard that protected the fighter's neck. But the helmet's small eyeholes made it difficult to find an opponent during combat.

MANICA
Manicas helped protect the warriors' sword arms.

OCREA
These leg guards covered a warrior's knees and shins.

MURMILLO

THIS GLADIATOR CLASS GOT ITS NAME FROM A FISH. THEIR LARGE HELMETS WERE OFTEN DECORATED WITH A FISH CREST.

HELMET

The big fin-like crest helped deflect blows to the head. The full-face grill protected the fighter's face from the sharp prongs of an opponent's trident.

SCUTUM

This big, curved shield was made from three layers of wood glued together and covered with leather. It was strong enough to deflect powerful blows from almost any weapon. But its 10-kilogram (22-pound) weight slowed gladiators down.

MANICA

A manica could be made of leather, cloth or metal. It was worn on the warrior's sword arm for protection.

OCREA

This metal leg guard covered the warrior's knee and shin. It protected the front of the gladiator's leg that wasn't covered by the scutum.

BALTEUS

This wide leather or metal belt was the only body protection these gladiators were allowed to wear. It protected a warrior's midsection from enemy weapons.

Lightweight gladiators included the *hoplomachus* and *retiarius*. These warriors carried few weapons and wore little armour. This exposed them more to attacks from heavily armoured opponents. But their light gear allowed them to run fast and make nimble attacks.

RETIARIUS

RETIARIUS MEANS "NET-FIGHTER". THESE GLADIATORS GOT THEIR NAME FROM THE WEIGHTED NETS THEY USED DURING BATTLES.

BAREHEADED
This gladiator type was the only one to go bareheaded into battle. By not wearing a heavy helmet, these fighters had great vision and could quickly dodge attacks. However, a single well-aimed blow could kill them.

GALERUS
This shoulder guard protected a fighter's left shoulder and upper arm. The metal absorbed the energy of a blow, while the curved upper plate helped deflect attacks.

BALTEUS
This wide leather belt helped protect a fighter's midsection from stabbing and cutting attacks.

MANICA
Swords and other sharp weapons could easily cut through leather manicas. To solve this problem, some gladiators boiled the leather in water and wax to make it harder and stronger.

HOPLOMACHUS

HELMET

The hoplomachus' helmet had a rounded top and wide, low brim. Its design helped deflect an enemy's sword before it could cause damage.

BALTEUS

This wide leather belt protected a fighter's midsection during battle.

MANICA

Like other gladiators, the hoplomachus wore a manica to protect his sword arm.

PARMULA

Hoplomachus gladiators fought with these small, round shields attached to their left arms. They were small, but strong and useful for deflecting blows.

OCREA

Because of their small shields, these gladiators needed better leg protection. They often wore padded wraps under metal plate armour. The metal plates helped deflect sword strikes, while the padding helped absorb the energy of a blow.

CHAPTER TWO

DEATH BY SCIENCE

Gladiators were trained in various fighting styles and used specific weapons for those styles. Their weapons used science in different ways to be effective in battle.

Heavy vs. light weapons

Heavyweight gladiators used mostly heavier weapons like swords and spears. The fighters knew how to use these weapons to create maximum **momentum** in an attack. When they hit another object, they created a heavy impact that could cause a lot of damage.

Lightweight gladiators relied on weapons that allowed for speed and **mobility**. Lightweight weapons like daggers could stab, thrust and cut quickly and effectively. Using these weapons, a lightweight fighter could make fast, deadly attacks before his opponent could strike back.

momentum amount of force in a moving object determined by the object's mass and speed

mobility ability to move quickly and easily

Most gladiators carried more than one weapon. If a warrior lost his main weapon, a smaller one was used as a back-up. Small weapons were good for close combat too.

As with armour, a gladiator's weapons were based on his weight class. Heavy weapons were strong and could do great damage. Light weapons were easy to handle and could be used to strike quickly.

THE GLADIUS

THE MOST FAMOUS WEAPON OF THE GLADIATOR WAS THE *GLADIUS*. THIS SHORT SWORD WAS USED MOSTLY BY HEAVYWEIGHT GLADIATORS. ITS KILLER REPUTATION CAME FROM THE SCIENCE OF ITS DESIGN. THE SWORD'S WIDE, THICK BLADE HELPED REDUCE THE AMOUNT OF **FORCE** NEEDED TO CUT THROUGH AN ENEMY. ITS SHORT LENGTH ALSO MADE IT EASY TO USE IN CLOSE COMBAT.

BLADE TIP
When stabbing with the gladius, the force of the blow was concentrated in the tip of the blade. This concentrated energy allowed the blade to pierce the enemy's armour and body.

BLADE WIDTH
The gladius' wide shape helped make it stronger and less likely to get bent in a fight.

BLADE LENGTH
The gladius' short length required a gladiator to add strength and speed to get a killing blow. Heavyweight fighters used their own strength, **mass** and arm speed to give the sword the necessary momentum for the kill. But lightweight gladiators had to run at an opponent to get the greatest momentum possible.

FACT

The word "gladiator" comes from the name of the sword, gladius.

force energy or strength

mass amount of material in an object

Weapon science

Gladiators used many kinds of weapons for arena fighting. Some weapons relied on weight and momentum to strike a deadly blow. Others were dangerous because of their speed and ability to quickly deal damage.

BOW AND ARROW

Sagittarius gladiators often fought with bows and arrows. A bow is a simple machine called a "two arm spring". When a warrior pulled back on the bowstring, the force was stored as **potential energy**. When he let go of the string, the energy became **kinetic energy** to let the arrow fly to its target.

SICA

The *sica* was a short, curved sword. Its blade was about 41 to 46 centimetres (16 to 18 inches) long. It focused the force of a blow into a small area. The curved shape also provided a better angle of attack, allowing more of the blade to hit the target.

NET AND TRIDENT

These were the weapons of retiarius gladiators. Heavy lead weights were knotted into the ropes of the net. When the retiarius threw the net, the weights increased the net's momentum to help it fly faster and farther.

Spearlike tridents were used for piercing enemies' bodies or poking out eyes. One prong was longer than the other to focus the force of a thrusting strike. Tridents were about 1.8 meters (6 feet) long. Their length allowed retiarius warriors to slash and cut at enemies from a greater distance.

SPEARS

Spears worked best at high speed. Gladiators gave a spear speed in two ways. One was by running while holding it. The faster he ran, the more force he could use to thrust the spear into his enemy. Gladiators sometimes threw spears instead. A warrior used his strength to hurl it with as much force as possible. The harder he threw the spear, the faster and farther it travelled.

FACT

Sometimes a gladiator's sword was purposely blunted before a fight. It takes more force to cut with a dull blade. This made the fight longer and more interesting for the crowds.

potential energy energy stored in an object, waiting to be released

kinetic energy energy of a moving object

CHAPTER THREE

TRAINING TO LIVE AND KILL

Weightlifting. Sprints. Running. Skipping. Modern athletes train with these exercises all the time. Gladiators did too. Gladiator training was all about physical fitness. They focused on improving their **agility**, strength and speed. They had to be in peak physical condition. Anything less meant almost certain death in the arena.

Weight class training

Gladiator trainees were divided based on their size. Large men were chosen to be heavyweight gladiators. They increased their strength and built muscle by lifting and carrying heavy objects. Other exercises included picking up other gladiators and swinging them around.

Smaller men usually became lightweight gladiators. These fighters focused on increasing their speed and endurance. They ran sprints, shadowboxed and hit bags filled with sand. They also practised their accuracy by throwing and catching a small ball while running.

agility ability to move in a quick and easy way

Daily training

Gladiators began their training by learning to wrestle each other. They learned grapples, holds, takedowns and other moves. Later they learned weapon skills by practising with wooden weapons. As their skills improved, they gradually moved up to training with real swords, spears, tridents and other weapons.

Regardless of their class, all gladiators trained to be stronger. Trainers used the idea of progressive overload to increase the warriors' strength. This type of training is done by gradually lifting more weight a little at a time. Over time the gladiators' muscles grew in strength and **stamina**.

Gladiators also needed to be able to move in combat. Agility and flexibility could mean the difference between victory and defeat. Trainees practised with a special machine that had high and low rotating poles. They had to jump and duck to avoid getting their heads or legs bashed by the poles. This training helped them to have faster reflexes during a fight.

FACT

Gladiators had their own energy drink. It was made from ashes and vinegar. This mix had a lot of calcium, which was believed to help remedy body pain.

stamina energy and strength to keep doing something for a long time

Putting training to the test

Gladiators needed good balance to be effective fighters. Every object has mass and a **centre of gravity**. A human's centre of gravity is usually slightly higher than the waist.

Nutrition was an important part of gladiator training. Gladiators ate mostly beans and grains. This protein-rich food helped them become strong and gave them the energy they needed for fighting.

SPEAR THROWING SCIENCE

Spears were useful weapons for gladiators. They allowed the warriors to attack opponents from a safe distance. Accurate spear throwing involved physics, as well as strength, agility, good balance and good aim.

1. The gladiator first judged the distance needed to throw the spear. Then he ran a short distance before throwing it. This added speed to the spear as he threw it, allowing it to travel farther.

centre of gravity point at which a person or object can balance

A heavyweight gladiator learned to keep his centre of gravity low by crouching or bending his knees. From this position he could move and attack without losing his balance. But a lightweight gladiator had to be fast on his feet while keeping his balance. Agility training helped him to control his centre of gravity and maintain his balance during a fight.

2 A gladiator had to throw a spear with the correct angle of attack to hit the target. If the angle was too high, it would fly over the target. If it angle was too low, the spear would fall short.

3 Success! The gladiator hit the target and is ready to use a spear in combat.

CHAPTER FOUR

STAYING ALIVE IN THE ARENA

The main strategy for gladiators in the arena was simple: don't lose. For a gladiator, losing a fight usually meant losing his life. There were few rules in the arena. Tricky moves and blows from behind were not allowed. But otherwise gladiators had to be ready for anything.

Mock battles

Gladiators didn't always fight one-on-one. Sometimes huge mock battles between gladiator "armies" filled the arena. During these battles, heavyweight gladiators often used a move called the "tortoise". They held up their shields to form a protective shell around them.

Gladiators didn't always fight other gladiators. Sometimes they fought wild and dangerous animals such as bulls, lions or tigers to entertain the crowd.

Lightweight gladiators spaced themselves around the edges of the group. Some hurled spears called *hastas* into a battle from a distance. Others used their speed and mobility to strike quickly and then back off. A few lightweight gladiators, known as *essedari*, fought with heavy spears from fast-moving chariots. The chariots' speed allowed the spears to be thrown far and fast.

 Fights between secutors and retiarii were very popular in ancient Rome. The two gladiator types had a perfect balance of speed and power against each other.

One-on-one strategies

One of the most popular gladiator match-ups was the retiarius vs. the secutor. The retiarius was popular because his weapons were so unusual. He could use his weighted net as a throwing weapon. But to be effective, he had to throw it at the correct **trajectory** to tangle up the secutor. He first swung it around to keep his enemy at a distance. He then tossed it at his enemy, hoping to tangle up his opponent's feet or weapons.

If the retiarius was successful with the net, he could then use his trident. The long weapon allowed him to attack from beyond the reach of the secutor's blade. He would use his speed to gain momentum and thrust the trident into his opponent's body.

The secutor's main strategy was to stay behind his shield and wait for the retiarius to get close. One way a secutor could take out the enemy's trident was to deflect an attack with his shield. Then when the enemy was off balance, he could make a counter attack. The secutor didn't need much speed for his attack. His strength combined with his sharp gladius would be enough to strike a killing blow.

trajectory path of an object as it flies through the air

projectile object that is thrown or shot through the air

Sword strategies

Most gladiators knew how to fight with a gladius. The warriors based their sword strategies on the opponents they faced and the weapons they used.

Thrusting

Thrusting attacks focused the force of the attack into the sword's sharp point. The warrior first crouched down to lower his centre of gravity. He then created momentum and force by jumping up and forward. Thrusting attacks were best for piercing enemy armour and flesh.

Cutting and slashing

The wide space in an arena provided a gladiator with plenty of room to swing his blade. This allowed him to put strength and speed into his attacks. Cutting and slashing attacks were best for fighting faster and lightly armoured opponents.

Entertaining the crowd

Gladiators might have been the rock stars of Rome, but they weren't soldiers. Their goal wasn't always to kill their enemies. Their job was to put on a good show for the crowd and the Emperor.

Running. Hitting. Cutting. Thrusting. Throwing. Gladiator fights were balanced with different science concepts to even the odds. One fighter was big and slow, but had heavy armour and weapons. Another had little protection, but was fast and could strike his enemy quickly. Whoever used science to his best advantage usually lived to fight another day.

GLOSSARY

agility   ability to move in a quick and easy way

centre of gravity   point at which a person or object can balance

deflect   to cause something to go in a different direction

disperse   to spread out over a wide area

force   energy or strength

kinetic energy   energy of a moving object

mass   amount of material in an object

mobility   ability to move quickly and easily

momentum   amount of force in a moving object determined by the object's mass and speed

physics   science that studies matter, energy, force and motion

potential energy   energy stored in an object, waiting to be released

projectile   object that is thrown or shot through the air

stamina   energy and strength to keep doing something for a long time

trajectory   path of an object as it flies through the air

Comprehension questions

1. Strength, force, movement and speed were all part of a gladiator's life. How do you use these science ideas in your life every day?

2. Heavyweight and lightweight gladiators used different types of weapons, armour and fighting styles. If you were a gladiator, which class would fit you best? What kinds of equipment would you have and how would you use it?

Books

A Heroic History of Gladiators and Ancient Warriors
(Blast Through the Past), Rachel Minay (Franklin Watts, 2016)

Clash of the Gladiators (DK Reads), Catherine Chambers
(DK Children, 2014)

Life as a Gladiator (You Choose: Warriors), Michael Burgan
(Raintree, 2015)

Websites

www.bbc.co.uk/history/ancient/romans/launch_gms_gladiator.shtml
Prepare a gladiator for battle in the arena in this game.

www.ducksters.com/history/ancient_roman_arena_entertainment.php
Learn more about the Roman Arena, where gladiators fought, on this website.

www.historyforkids.net/ancient-rome.html
Discover Ancient Rome through gladiators, Roman science, daily life and more.